DANGEROUS MAMMALS

TIGERS

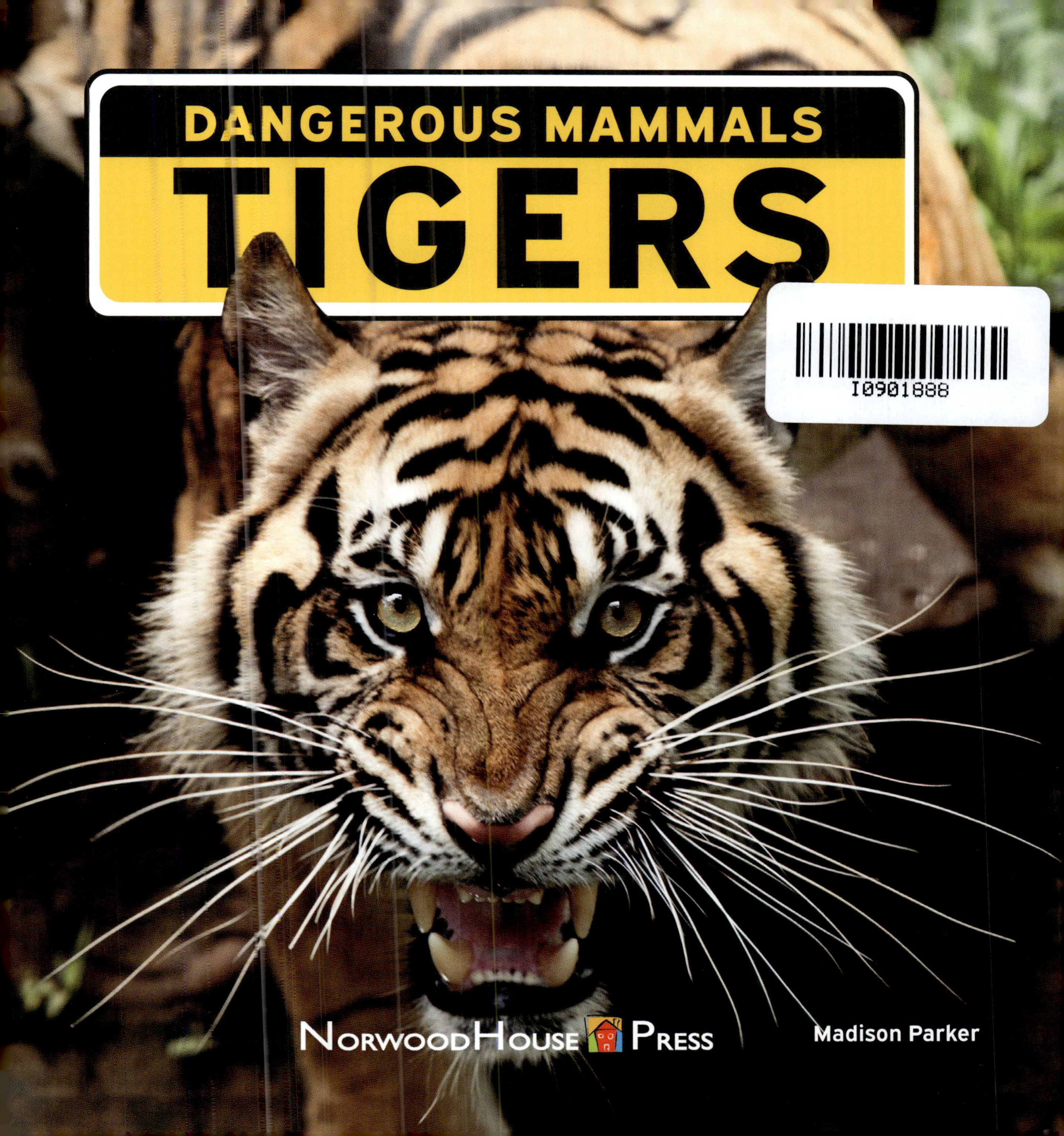

I0901888

NorwoodHouse Press

Madison Parker

Library of Congress Cataloging-in-Publication Data:

Names: Parker, Madison.
Title: Tigers / Madison Parker.
Description: Buffalo, NY : Norwood House Press, 2025. | Series: Dangerous mammals | Includes glossary and index.
Identifiers: ISBN 9781684502684 (pbk.) | ISBN 9781684502691 (library bound) | ISBN 9781684502707 (ebook)
Subjects: LCSH: Tiger--Juvenile literature.
Classification: LCC QL737.C23 P375 2025 | DDC 599.756--dc23

Published in 2025 by
Norwood House Press
2544 Clinton Street
Buffalo, NY 14224

Copyright © 2025 Norwood House Press

Designer: Ocean Books
Editor: Kim Thompson

Photo credits: Cover, pp. 1, 8 JFS07/Shutterstock.com; p. 5 Nitish Madan; p. 6 Gayamal Rathnavibusjana/Shutterstock.com; p. 7 Ondrej Prosicky/Shutterstock.com; p. 10 Nachalitl/Shutterstock.com; p. 11 canghai76/Shutterstock.com; p. 12 kksteven12/Shutterstock.com; p. 13 Sigit Adhi Wibowo; p. 14 Gudkov Andrey/Shutterstock.com; p. 15 dptro/Shutterstock.com; p. 17 pmvtisl/Shutterstock.com; p. 18 Sourabd Bharti/Shutterstock.com; p. 21 Setta Sornnoi/Shutterstock.com

All rights reserved. No part of this book may be reproduced in any form without permission in writing from the publisher, except by a reviewer.

Printed in the United States of America

Some of the images in this book illustrate individuals who are models. The depictions do not imply actual situations or events.

CPSIA compliance information: Batch #CW25NHP: For further information contact Norwood House Press at 1-800-237-9932.

Find us on

TABLE OF CONTENTS

MEET THE TIGER

Tigers are big cats with orange fur and black stripes. They are **mammals**. Mother tigers feed their babies milk.

TYPES OF TIGERS

Bengal tigers live in India and other parts of South Asia. They can be dangerous when they feel **threatened**.

The Siberian tiger is also called the Amur tiger. It has thick fur for cold weather. This cat lives in parts of Russia and China. It is big and strong, which makes it dangerous.

Sumatran tigers are small. Their stripes are thick and dark. They live only on the island of Sumatra in Indonesia. These tigers can be dangerous if their **territory** is disturbed.

The Indochinese tiger has light fur and only a few stripes. It lives in Southeast Asia. These tigers are **elusive**, but they can be dangerous if met face-to-face.

The rare South China tiger is one of the smallest tigers. It is found mostly in zoos. If these cats feel trapped, they can be **aggressive**.

The Malayan tiger has dark fur. It lives in Southeast Asia. These tigers are strong. They can be dangerous when they are protecting their babies.

The Javan tiger lived on the island of Java in Indonesia, but it is now **extinct**. It had long whiskers and many stripes. Javan tigers were quick and powerful hunters.

FAVORITE FOODS

Tigers are **predators**. They hunt large animals like deer and wild boars. They can eat 40 pounds (18 kilograms) of meat in one day.

Tigers also hunt smaller animals like rabbits and birds. They use their sharp claws and teeth to catch **prey**. They are good at sneaking up quietly.

Tigers are good swimmers.
Sometimes, they catch fish in rivers.

STAYING SAFE AROUND TIGERS

If you see a tiger, stay calm. Do not run. Running might make the tiger chase you. Keep looking at the tiger as you slowly move away.

Never feed a tiger or get too close. Watch from a safe distance.

If a tiger seems aggressive, make loud noises. Try to make your body look bigger by standing tall and waving your arms. This might make the tiger go away.

GLOSSARY

aggressive (uh-GRES-iv): threatening; ready to attack

elusive (i-LOO-siv): very hard to find or capture; shy

extinct (ik-STINGKT): no longer found alive; known about only through fossils or history

mammals (MAM-uhlz): animals that are warm-blooded, that have hair or fur, that usually give birth to live babies, and that produce milk to feed their babies

predators (PRED-uh-turz): animals that live by hunting other animals for food

prey (pray): animals that are hunted by other animals for food

territory (TER-i-tor-ee): an area that is occupied and defended by an animal and that often contains the animal's nest, den, or home

threatened (THRE-tuhnd): in danger of being harmed

THINKING QUESTIONS

1. Why are tigers mammals?
2. What kinds of food do tigers like to eat?
3. What should you do if you see a tiger?
4. How are the Bengal tiger and the Indochinese tiger alike and different?
5. Where do tigers live?

INDEX

ABOUT THE AUTHOR

Madison Parker spent her childhood in the city of Chicago, Illinois. A farm girl at heart, today she lives in Wisconsin with her husband and four children on a small farm with cows, goats, chickens, and two miniature horses named Harley and David. Her favorite dessert is vanilla frozen custard with rainbow sprinkles, even in the winter.